My Little Tin Horn

Memories of being a kid during the 1930's and 1940's

Shelton R. McKeever

This book is for my children:
Michael
Lisa
Marc
Scott
Gregory
And for my stepdaughter
Jacquelyn

It is dedicated to my wife
Rita
Whose love, support, and guidance
Have sustained me for many years.

It is in memory of
Jack Newcomer
Who was the husband of the "Little
Brown-Haired Girl"
who chased me around the classroom in the
Fourth grade.

FOREWARD

This is a collection of memorable events when I was a kid.

Growing up during the 1930's and 1940's was a challenging and happy time when I learned to enjoy the simple things in life. It was also a time when each family was fending for itself and helping those families whose fathers were away at war. There were concerns and worries for the men of our family and other families.

Because we lived on a farm, we were able to grow and raise our own food. We had no electricity or telephone. A battery powered radio was used sparingly to keep up with the news.

Although we had a car, it was rarely used due to the shortage and rationing of gasoline. The only people in the area who used vehicles were the postman and a farmer who owned a cattle truck that served the area.

When we traveled to nearby places, we walked, rode horseback or rode on a horse-drawn wagon.

When we needed to see a doctor or have business in the closest town, we either hitched a ride with the mail carrier or hired the cattle truck.

The water supply was from a shallow well that had a line and hand pump in the kitchen. Water was heated on a wood-burning stove.

In the winter we took one bath a week. However, during the summer a daily swim in the creek was the order of the day.

I began doing farm chores when I was about six years old. This consisted of helping feed the livestock, weeding the garden, and hoeing the cornfield. In the fall, I helped harvest the corn and wheat.

After the war, we moved to a large farm located about two miles from a small town. The school there was larger and afforded me the opportunity to make friends with a number of other children. Too, the farm work was much more extensive than I had previously experienced.

Working on the farm during summers with extreme heat and winter with bitter cold forged my future. I decided that there were better ways to make a living.

As a first step, I realized that an education was a necessity. I was fortunate during my teen years to have teachers who made school interesting. This gave me the "springboard" to seek and acquire an advanced education.

My Maternal Grandparents house where I was born. This house started out as a log cabin, and was added onto with the birth of each of their children.

My Mother Hazel and Father Ray soon after they were married.

CHAPTER 1

Before World War II

Shelton R. McKeever

THE HORN

My earliest recollection was when I was about 3 or 4 years old. My parents took me to the local school to visit Santa Claus. After the visit they tried to point out the sleigh and reindeer on top of the building. I tried very hard to see them but was unable to do so.

That Christmas I received a little tin horn and drum. I really loved those instruments and spent a lot of time playing them and marching around the house. I must have created an awful lot of noise while doing this.

One day, a month or two after Christmas, I was feeling musically inclined. I searched high and low and could not find my instruments. In fact, I never found them.

Looking back, I remember my mother and father only half-heartedly helping me look.

It was many years later, when I had children of my own, that I realized what had happened to them.

The result of the loss of my instruments is that today I have no musical talent whatsoever.

1

THE HOUSE KEY

An incident occurred during the time I had the instruments which may have led to their demise. After returning from a visit to my grandparents, my father realized that he had forgotten the house key and that we were locked out.

My father discovered that a back window was unlocked but it was over seven feet above ground level and out of reach to him. However, he came up with a workable plan to get in the house. He used a long stick with which he was able to raise the window. He told me that he was going to lift me up and through the window and I was to go to the front door and unlock it.

It was a good plan but he did not know that inside the window on the floor was my little tin horn. I immediately became more interested in music than unlocking the front door.

It was some time later when my father came in (somewhat red-faced) and gave me the first of many lectures.

THE STREAKER

The first streaker I ever knew was me. I remember some of what happened but my mother filled in the details.

One warm spring day I had the desire to run nude through the neighborhood. It was a great feeling to run through the warm spring air after a long, cold winter.

With my clothes off I ran past my mother who was in the backyard hanging clothes on the line.

I remember the look on her face as I passed by. She stood there with something half on the line, her mouth agape and her eyes opened as wide as saucers.

She was so surprised and I was about twenty yards away before she made an attempt to catch me. What a sight we must have been as I ran out of the yard and down the alley.

My mother's yelling got the attention of a neighbor lady who blocked my path. I was caught but I really enjoyed my brief freedom in the warm air.

THE ROOSTER

When my first brother was born, I was sent to my grandmother's house (for safekeeping I suppose). While there I developed a fondness for helping her collect the chicken eggs from the hen house. At the same time, her rooster developed a fondness for chasing me.

Every day it was the same thing. I would go to the back yard gate. I would look one way then the other and make a mad dash to the hen house. On the way back, there stood that rooster between the yard gate and me. If memory serves me right, he was smiling. When he made his move, up to the top of the woodpile I would go, screaming all the way.

Thank God my grandmother always came to my rescue within a few minutes.

This chasing went on for months - every time I visited my grandmother. He would not bother anyone else, including my sister and cousins. He had my number and he knew it.

Sometime later we visited my grandmother and she said we were having that rooster for dinner. I really enjoyed that meal and it was my turn to smile.

Shelton R. McKeever

CHANGES

Upon returning home after the birth of my brother, I found several changes had occurred. My bedroom had been given to my baby brother and my bed had been moved to the storeroom. (This gave me a chance to look once again for my little tin horn.)

Another change was that my father had hired a housekeeper. She may have been a good housekeeper but she was a terrible cook. Had it been the other way around, she would have kept the job longer.

The final straw came when my father discovered she could not tell the difference between sugar and salt. That was the only time I remember having my oatmeal sweetened with salt.

MUSIC

In those years, my father owned and operated a grocery store/service station/pool room/beer garden that was located at the foot of the hill below our house.

I have memories of sitting with my mother at night. We sat in our dark living room listening to radio music while waiting for my father to come home. I believe that is when I developed a love of semi-classical and popular music of the 20's and 30's.

Shelton R. McKeever

THE POPSICLE

One day, as my mother was cooking, I climbed on a chair beside the stove to see what was in the kettle. Suddenly, the chair collapsed. I fell on the hot stove and burned my hand.

The screams were heard at my father's grocery store/service station/pool hall/ beer garden and he came running. After some consoling, he said that a Popsicle might ease the pain. He was right. Within minutes the pain was gone.

A few hours later, when I remembered how the Popsicle tasted, the pain and crying returned.

Where is my popsicle?

GREAT-GRANDMOTHER

I remember my great-grandmother coming to visit. She was Dutch and wore clothes of the "old country". This was usually a floor-length black dress and a bonnet.

I think the way she dressed scared me so I would run and hide. If I knew she was coming, I would post myself at the window in order to get an early start on hiding.

My favorite hiding place was under the bed with the "goblins" that I considered less scary than my great grandmother.

MOVE TO A SMALL FARM

There came a time when my parents announced my father's business had been sold and that we were moving to a small farm. This was the beginning of a new phase of my life.

CHAPTER 2

During World War II

WORLD WAR II

In retrospect, our move to the farm came at an opportune time. My father bought the farm in the fall and was to turn his business over to the new owner on January 1st. One Sunday in December my father came home from the business early and announced to my mother that the Japanese had attacked Pearl Harbor.

This was a very traumatic time for all of my family. My father and my uncles were of the age that was subject to being drafted into the armed services.

As it turned out, my father was above the maximum age and was never drafted. Several uncles were either drafted or volunteered. They all served overseas. One uncle was wounded while in Italy.

Even though the war had started, we continued with the move to the farm.

THE FARM

Let me describe the location of the farm. It was located across a large creek from an unpaved road. The creek ran in a north to south direction and was an excellent fishing stream.

We had neighbors to the north and to the south of us. Also, there was a neighbor to the east and across the creek from us. The National Forest was located to the west and adjoined our property.

Our water supply came from a shallow, rock-lined well that had been dug by hand. There was a hand pump and basin in the kitchen. During the summer we used a rope to lower milk and butter into the well to keep them cool.

There was no electricity. Our contact with the outside world was through the Sunday newspaper and a battery-operated radio.

When President Roosevelt had his "fireside chats" on the radio some of our neighbors would join us to listen to him. This would conserve their battery power because it was difficult to purchase batteries during the war.

MEMORIES

I have good memories of life on the farm during the "war years". Goods were scarce and were rationed by the government. The government issued coupons for food and goods. Coupons were issued for each family member.

One of the scarce things was the metal in toothpaste containers. When we bought toothpaste, the old tube had to be returned.

We had little money but by living on a farm we raised our own food and were able to supply beef cattle for the war effort. We were financially poor then but I have rich memories of that time.

In the winter we sat by the fireplace while my father read from the Bible or from a Zane Gray novel. Sometimes we roasted Irish potatoes or sweet potatoes (yams) in the fire and ate them while listening to our father.

I remember listening to FDR's fireside chats, the Grand Ole Opry and "Lum and Abner" on the battery radio. Even though I was not allowed to use the radio, I sometimes sneaked and listened to "Sky King", "Let's Pretend", "Sergeant Preston" and "Terry and the Pirates".

When the warmth of spring arrived I would take off my shoes and race across the meadow. What an experience that was!

Our house sat on a small bluff overlooking a creek. I would walk barefoot along the graveled creek bed. That is also an experience hard to forget because the gravel was painful on my feet. However, my feet toughened. By fall, I was able to run over gravel as fast as I did in the meadow.

THE FIRE

One cool Saturday in the fall my family and I were gathering walnuts. We left my young brother in a crib by the fireplace inside the house. For some reason, my mother went to check on him. She found that an ember had caught the house on fire.

My father, mother and sister grabbed buckets to get water from the creek. My father told me to run to a neighbor's about a half-mile away and get help.

I ran across our field, climbed a fence and raced across another field to the neighbor's house. I found the neighbor at his barn where he was feeding his cattle and told him our house was on fire. For some reason, he thought I was making up a story.

He said to let him finish up his chore and we could go in his house and have some of the cookies his wife had just made. I immediately forgot about the fire.

After about the second or third cookie I convinced him that we should go help put out the fire.

When we got back to our house the fire was out. My father wanted to know where I had been and I replied that I had been eating cookies.

STARTING SCHOOL

I entered a one-room school just after I turned six years old. The school was located about one mile from our house and one teacher taught grades 1 through 8.

My reputation preceded me and, for a few months, I was handicapped by it and teased by the other students.

Let me explain.

The prior year a nurse had come to each schoolhouse in the county to vaccinate the children starting school the next year.

I believe there were four of us lined up to get our shots (a boy, a girl, me and another boy). The first boy yelled "You are killing me!" when he got his shot.

No way were they going to kill me so I was gone. Back through the schoolhouse and out the door I went. Across the road and through the woods to the creek; down the creek to an escarpment where I hid while the entire school turned out to find me. They never did.

After a couple of hours, I walked back home where I was "convinced" that I needed to go to another school that afternoon and get my shots. I did.

GETTING TO SCHOOL

There were four of us in the first grade: three boys and one girl. There were about thirty of us in school from grades 1 through 8.

We all walked to school. Some walked from the south for as much as 2 miles and some walked from the north for about the same distance. During that time, schools were located about 4 miles apart. I was lucky because I walked only one mile from the north.

There were several ways of crossing the creek to get to the road. Normally, my father would take me across in a pole boat. Sometimes he would ride me across on one of his horses. Many times during the winter I could walk across on the ice.

The one-room schoolhouse where I completed grades 1 – 3.

SWINGING BRIDGE

There were times of floods when it was impossible to cross as stated above. Then, my father would walk me down the creek bank for about one and a half miles to a neighboring farm that had a "swinging bridge". We would cross the bridge and I would walk north about one half mile to school. I would retrace this path after school.

Those that have never crossed a "swinging bridge" have missed a lot of excitement. Two poles on each end anchor the bridge. Two large cables are strung between the poles. Vertical support cables are strung below these large ones. The vertical cables hold wooden boards. As you walk over the boards the bridge sways from side to side - thus a "swinging bridge".

Crossing one of the bridges for the first time can be a scary experience. I don't believe I ever got used to it.

MILKWEED PODS

In the fall our school undertook a project to collect milkweed pods. They would be used to make life preservers for our troops.

I had picked about four bags of the pods. When it came time to take them to school I could not find one of the bags. About a month later I found it but most of the pods were rotted. My father insisted that I take them to school anyway.

Years later I pictured some unfortunate sailor in the ocean wearing a stinking lifejacket and having to make the decision to put up with the odor or to take it off and sink.

ICE WATER

One evening as I was returning from school, my father came to give me a ride across the creek on the horse. It was winter. The snow was blowing and there was thin ice on the creek.

About halfway across the horse bucked and threw both of us off. Needless to say, both of us were wet and very cold. My father was also very angry.

Upon changing clothes he wanted to take his rifle and shoot the horse but was persuaded by my mother not to do it.

GAMES AT SCHOOL

During noon hour at school we had several games that were popular.

In winter we played a game called "the fox and the geese". This involved laying out a large circle in the snow with an "X' in the middle. Someone was named the "fox" and would chase the others. When a "goose" was tagged, that person became the "fox". The geese were safe when standing on one point or center of the "X".

In the fall and spring we played softball. The distances between bases varied. It was a very short distance to 1st base but a very long distance from 3rd to home plate. This made it easy to get a hit but hard to score. (Maybe this should be made the standard today).

Another game we played was called "Anthony Over". This involved throwing a soft ball over the roof of the schoolhouse. If someone on the other side caught it they were safe. If the ball wasn't caught, the kid that missed it went over to the other side. The game was over when there was no one on one side of the schoolhouse. I believe this was an original game to the school and was named after the nearby creek (Anthony's Creek).

THE FIGHT

When I entered the 2nd grade my sister entered the 1st grade and the two of us walked to school together. Sometime during the fall she and one of the boys in my class got into a fight. I quickly took her place and continued the fight into and over a coal pile. (The coal was used in a "pot-bellied" stove to heat the schoolhouse.) We created quite a mess when our clothes got covered in coal dust.

Our teacher intervened. She made me and the other boy sit in the schoolhouse while she guarded the front door.

At this point, I should mention that the building had two back windows. It didn't take long for the other boy and me to resolve our differences and make use of a back window to continue our noontime playing.

THE LITTLE BLONDE-HAIRED GIRL

After beginning the 2nd grade the little blonde-haired girl in my class and I did the 3rd grade studies along with our regular studies. This involved two sets of homework and tests. At the end of the year we were passed to the 4th grade. That is how I managed to be two years ahead of my sister throughout our schooling.

By the way, I thought that the little blonde-haired girl was "cute". I was only seven years old but I knew "cute" when I saw it.

FIRST DATE

During this time, many of my fellow student's fathers were in the armed forces. The women were left to raise the children and to do the farm work. The men remaining in the community would join together and help those families with their farm work.

One day my father, along with several other men, went to help the blonde-haired girl's mother because her father was overseas. She asked me to go home with her after school that day and explained that I could return with my father when he went home. For some reason I liked the idea and agreed to do so.

I told my sister that I was going home with the little blonde girl and that she would have to walk home by herself. This brought on a "sister fit" and I chased her a short distance so she would do it.

The little blonde girl lived about two miles south of the school. Many of the students lived in this direction but she lived the greatest distance away. On the way down the road, many of the students (especially the 7th and 8th graders) teased us. At the time I wondered why.

We were almost to her house when we met my father and several other men on their way home. I joined them. It seems as though they all were in hysterics at catching me with her. I saw nothing funny but I realized that they were making fun of me.

I never visited another girl at her home until I was about 18 years old.

BIG GAME HUNTER

A cougar began killing some of the farmers' cattle and sheep. On several occasions, they went hunting for the animal but to no avail.

My brother was about five. He and I formulated a plan to do our own hunting using BB guns that our uncles had recently given us. After school, we started on our trek through the snow. Into the forest and up a winding trail we went. That became the first successful hunt of my life.

As we were going up the trail we heard a bloodcurdling scream. In a fraction of a second we both realized that a BB gun would not do the job.

We did not take the long way home. Straight as an arrow and fast as a bullet we went toward our home. Upon reaching a fence that divided our pasture from the forest, I took a sliding dive and went under it. My brother could not and began yelling "Help Me", "Help Me". After peeking over my shoulder and discovering that the cougar was not chasing us, I went back and helped him.

THE DUEL

BB gun ammunition was scarce during that time. My father was able to buy ten packages that my brother and I divided.

We had heard about cowboys having duels so we decided we would have one. We started out back to back and were to take ten paces, turn and fire. At about pace six I became worried that he might beat me. So, at pace eight, I turned and aimed at the back of his head. When he reached pace ten he turned and I fired.

We were both very lucky. My shot only grazed the top of his head but he started crying and threatened to tell our parents.

It cost me two packages of BB's to bribe him not to tell.

BIRD KILL

After shooting at many birds with my BB gun, I finally managed to kill one.

I went to pick it up and was suddenly overcome with guilt. I remembered the words of my mother who said that God sees everything you do. I thought that if God sees everything, he would not like to see me kill the bird.

Instead of being proud of my shot, I was ashamed. I did not tell anyone what I had done.

INVENTING PROFANITY

One of my chores during the summer months was to mow the lawn. Our lawn mower was a reel-type push mower (In those days a power mower was unheard of).

These mowers would often get jammed with grass clippings, especially if the grass was damp and/or high.

One Saturday evening just before sunset my parents reminded me that the lawn needed to be mowed.

I got the lawnmower and started to work. After a couple of laps around the yard the inevitable happened. The blades were jammed with grass clippings.

I stopped mowing and began to clear the blades when I noticed my sister approaching. I quickly reminded her not to push the mower while I was working on the blades.

The next thing I knew she gave the mower a shove while my hand was in the blades. There I was dancing around the yard holding my bloody hand and yelling "Old Man Gallagher".

I never heard this profanity before or after.

SNAKE BITE

There were several piles of rocks along the creek bank. Many times my parents had warned us children to stay away from the rocks because snakes had been seen nearby. One day, I was attracted to a large flat rock near the bottom of one pile. I knelt and lifted the rock. Immediately I was struck on the knee by a snake.

I was afraid to tell my parents about what happened because I feared their scolding (or spanking). Soon afterwards my mother called us for dinner (lunch).

While having dinner, I looked down at my knee and found it to be three or four times bigger than normal. This scared me because I realized that the snake had been poisonous. Then, I had to tell my mother what had happened.

My father was not home so my mother had to administer first aid. If I remember right, she applied a turpentine compress. When my father got home late that evening, the swelling had gone down.

In retrospect, I was lucky that the snake had bit my knee and the fangs had not penetrated. Also, I have never heard of using turpentine to treat snakebite.

SISTER BITE

My sister would often get angry with me. Her weapon of choice was her teeth, which she sank into the calf of my leg. I would go to my mother dragging my sister along and say, "She is doing it again".

This went on for many months. Finally, my mother told my sister that she should come to her and that she would punish me. Actually, my mother just pronounced my sentence. My father carried out the punishment.

I don't know what hurt worse, a sore butt or a sore leg.

My Sister and I at a time when we were not fighting!

THE SWIMMING LESSON

A large, deep water hole was located on the creek near our house. This water hole was used for fishing and swimming.

This is where an uncle taught me to swim. It was easy for him. While I was standing on the bank, he picked me up, threw me in and said, "Swim". Somehow I did.

BOATING

My father made a flat bottom pole boat for crossing the creek. I often used it to retrieve the mail from the box on the opposite side.

I tried to do this one time when the creek was flooding. I quickly learned that it is hard to navigate a pole boat in swift water. When I got across, I was about one hundred yards downstream of where I wanted to be.

On the way back, I pulled the boat along the bank for about one hundred yards above the landing on the other side and made it back OK.

UNCLE'S MOTORCYCLE

One of my uncles bought a motorcycle during his late teens and would often visit us. Once or twice he gave me a ride on it. I was so impressed that I promised myself to get one when I was old enough.

One day I heard my parents talking about my uncle. It seemed as though he had an accident while riding his motorcycle on a gravel road. They said that he would need to sleep on his stomach for several weeks until the skin on his rear end grew back.

This caused me to change my promise to: "I will never get a motorcycle".

TROUT FISHING

Trout season opened in mid-March. My father and a couple of uncles had planned a fishing trip about five miles upstream from our house. After much begging and pleading, they agreed to take me along. The weather on that day was cold (about freezing), dark and overcast.

We parked my uncle's car on the road above the creek. My father and I went downhill to the stream and began fishing. At the same time, one uncle went upstream and the other went downstream.

Ice was covering the creek near it banks. At some point, I decided to go a short distance upstream and fish from a log into a pool below. Soon I had a strike and jerked the fishing pole to set the hook! Let me mention that the log was covered with ice.

My father looked up when he heard the splash and saw my hat floating in the water.

I was half frozen when he pulled me out. It took my father several minutes to find my uncle and retrieve the car keys to take me home.

I ran up and down the road to keep warm before he got back with the keys.

That was the end of my first trout fishing trip.

FISH FOR DINNER

Every once in a while my mother would ask me to go catch some fish for dinner. Sometimes I could catch enough for dinner. Sometimes I could not.

Once I had caught only a few, and some neighbors offered to show me how to always catch enough. We went to the creek, picked up some large stones and began wading upstream. When we saw a fish go under a rock, we threw the stone on top of the rock the fish was hiding under. This would stun the fish and it would float to the top of the water.

After that, I was always able to get enough fish for dinner. However, I had to stay alert to be sure the game warden would not catch me.

STRONG NEIGHBOR

Our neighbor, who owned the land across the creek from us, was an interesting character. He was just short of seven feet tall and weighed over three hundred pounds.

I remember him telling the story of his escape from the Atlanta Federal Prison where he was serving time for making moonshine whiskey. He and several other prisoners escaped one Sunday morning when their cell doors were unlocked for them to hear church services. He hid in a water-filled ditch just outside the prison walls while police searched everywhere else. After dark he left the area and ended up in West Virginia. He was never recaptured and went back to his previous work before becoming a preacher.

My father told about discussing this man with a sheriff in the area. The sheriff knew the man was making moonshine but they could never catch him.

His still was located on the Virginia-West Virginia border. When the law officers approached from one state, he just moved it to the other. The sheriff said that one time they had a coordinated effort with Virginia officers. When he crossed to the West Virginia side, they started after him through the snow. Even though he was carrying a keg of moonshine they were not able to catch him. They found only one place where he set the keg down and rested during the six or seven mile chase.

I was witness to the man's strength. The gate to his field was located directly across the creek from our house. One winter I watched as he brought several loads of hay to his cattle with a tractor pulled wagon. There was a slight downgrade from the field to the road. On the return trip he would let the tractor and wagon coast downhill while he jumped off, ran ahead and opened the gate. After the tractor and wagon went through, he would close the gate, run and catch them and go for another load.

It got my attention when the gate got stuck during one trip. To keep the tractor from crashing through the gate, he got in front of it, put his back on the tractor and stopped it. That was no task for a weakling.

CLEARING LAND

During one winter, my father cleared two areas of land to provide for more pasture and farm land. These areas were mostly brush-covered but did include several trees. The trees were sawed down and cut up using a handsaw. They were then split for firewood. The brush was cut, piled and burned.

It was my job to burn the brush on Saturdays and in the evenings after school. It felt good to be near the fire during cold weather but this is where I learned that smoke comes after you - no matter which side of the fire you are on.

CATCHING RABBITS

Mowing hay required that the mower go around and around the hay field beginning on the outside. This resulted in all the animal life being driven to the inside.

When the job was nearly done, many animals were scared out of the tall grass. Most of these animals were rabbits. I liked to be there when this happened so I could chase them over the newly mown hay. They could not run as fast over the cut hay as they did otherwise so I was able to catch them. This was all for fun and I would let them go after I caught them.

Shelton R. McKeever

BUCKING HORSE

One summer my sister, brother and I were helping in the hay field. We rode a horse that pulled a sled to pick up hay shocks. We would then drag them to a place for stacking. This was the same horse that had thrown my father and me into the icy creek the previous winter.

All of a sudden the horse began bucking and running across the field. It threw my sister and brother off. I had the harness wrapped around my feet and stayed on for a few minutes until I became scared and jumped off.

My father wanted to whip the horse but he was afraid my mother would intervene.

BALKING HORSES

While I'm on the subject of the horse: One winter my father and I were taking a load of hay to cattle in the pasture field. The team of horses stalled and acted as though they could not pull such a heavy load.

After several minutes of trying to get them going, my father slid off the wagon and pulled the pin that hooked the tongue to the wagon. Once again, my father tried to get the team to move. Still they acted as though the load was too heavy even though there was nothing for them to pull. They were faking it. A few years later the horses were sold.

LOSING A SISTER

When the wheat, or oats, or barley was ready for harvest, someone in the area who owned a thrashing machine would travel from farm to farm to thrash the grain. Farmers in the community would band together and travel from farm to farm to help each other.

One fall, the day after our wheat was thrashed and the thrashing machine had moved on to the next farm, my brother and I decided it would be a great sport to jump out the barn window into a huge pile of straw. This was great fun until my sister decided to join us.

On her first jump she did not slide down the pile as my brother and I had done. Instead she hit the straw as though it was a pool of water. She disappeared into the pile.

My brother and I decided that we should dig her out otherwise we would be scolded for losing our sister.

LOST BROTHER

One cool winter afternoon my brother came up missing. A full-scale search was made of our house. We searched from the attic to the basement...no brother. We then searched outside from the well to the granary, to the chicken house, to the barn.

Down to the creek we went. My father and sister went upstream. My mother and I went downstream. No brother was found.

When we assembled back at the house, my father and mother were discussing the idea of getting our neighbors and the sheriff to help. I looked under the kitchen stove and found my brother. He had curled up in the warm area and fallen asleep.

TAKING GRAIN TO THE MILL

After the fall harvest we would take grain to the closest mill, which was about twenty miles away. The wheat would be milled into flour and bran. Corn would be ground into meal and "cracked corn".

The mill was located on a river and water power was used to run the operation. The mill owner would take a percentage of the product as his fee.

The machinery fascinated me. Water ran over the drive wheel that turned the rod from which gears, pulleys and chains operated everything.

MAKING SYRUP

With the help of a neighbor, we made our own maple syrup and sorghum molasses.

When the first warm days of spring came we inserted "taps" in the maple trees and began collecting sap. Small buckets were attached to the wooden taps. On the average, we would need to visit each tree two or three times a day to pour the sap into larger containers. When it became unusually warm, we were constantly going from tree to tree.

The sap was boiled in large containers and reduced to about one tenth of the original volume. It was a lot of work but well worth it when the syrup was poured over pancakes.

We grew sorghum cane for use in making molasses. In the fall we would go through the field and strip all the leaves from the cane. Then we would harvest the cane stalks by using a cane cutter (a type of scythe) and pile the stalks on a horse pulled wagon. When a full load was reached the cane was taken to a neighbor who owned a cane press and syrup boiler.

The sap was extracted by using horse power to press the sap. The horse was hitched to a pole that was pulled in a circle to drive the grinder and press. Sap was collected from this machine and taken to a large pan evaporator. The pan (actually more than one pan) was about fifteen feet long, five feet wide and about two feet deep.

A wood fire was used underneath the pans to heat them to a boil. Once the sap was boiling, we had to constantly remove the debris and impurities by using a skimmer.

This was at least a two day process and someone had to be there day and night to keep the fire going and to skim the syrup. At that time I did not like sorghum molasses and considered this to be unrewarding work. Because of this, I was bored and often fell asleep when it was my time to tend the evaporator. When this happened, I was "reminded" of my duties.

CHRISTMAS TIME

As it is with all kids, Christmas was very special. The first big event was to follow my father through the snow as he pulled a sled to the woods. There we would search for the "perfect" tree. After sawing it down, my father would tie it to the sled and pull it back to our house.

That evening the whole family would join in decorating the tree. The decorations were simple: consisting of garland, tinsel, a few ornaments, and of course, the angel on top.

We always went to bed early on Christmas Eve, so that we could get up early and see what Santa had brought. We kids usually got up before daylight.

Once we got up too early. We rushed into the living room to find that Santa had not been there yet. My parents insisted that we had to sleep longer in order for Santa to get there.

Christmas presents during the war years were usually very sparse. We would receive jigsaw puzzles, coloring books, small-recycled rubber toys and the like. I remember one Christmas when I received my own hoe and bucket to use when helping in the garden. The grandest gift was when I received my own pocketknife.

TOYS

In addition to the toys listed previously, I had homemade toys.

My father made a checkerboard and checkers. This occupied a lot of time, especially during the winter months.

A slingshot was made from a Y-shaped tree branch and a piece of rubber from an old inner tube. Gravel was used as ammunition.

I used a hollow reed to make a bean shooter. You would stick a bean in one end and blow through the reed. The same reed could be used to make a flute.

Cutting a thread spool in half and running a stick through the center hole made a "whirly gig".

A "pea shooter" was made from a clothespin. You used one half of the clothespin and the spring. The spring would be pulled back and a pea lay on top. When the spring was pulled, it would shoot the pea forward. Sometimes the spring would slip and pinch my hand.

I made a "whirly gig" by using a large button and a string. The string was looped through two eyes of the button and the ends tied. My thumbs were hooked over the end loops. Pulling the loops started the button spinning and the harder I pulled the faster the button spun.

One summer my father made me a pair of stilts from two long, slender pieces of wood. They took some "getting used to" but once this was done, I enjoyed walking and running on them.

Once I helped my father make a kite from a large piece of wrapping paper and wood splints. It took about half a day to finish the project and the wind about ten minutes to destroy it.

Shelton R. McKeever

THE SWING

During the summer, my father would make a swing by hanging two ropes over a limb of a large sugar maple tree that grew in our front yard. My sister and I discovered that jumping off the swing while it was in motion allowed us to fly for some distance. One day we had a contest to see who could fly farther.

She jumped first. I decided to show her up by jumping in the opposite direction over the yard fence.

I did not make it.

CHURCH

From time to time we attended a church that was about one and one half miles south of our house.

During the war, preachers were in short supply and one preacher would have four or five churches to administer. This meant that services at our church were held only about once a month.

During one service, when the collection plate was passed, I thought that they were passing out money so I helped myself. This earned me a slap on the hand by my mother.

I still get nervous in church when the collection plate is passed because I can still remember that slap.

PATERNAL GRANDFATHER

My paternal grandfather was a tall, slender man that I considered to be distinguished looking. He was a retired schoolteacher and farmer. He raised twelve children that included eight sons and four daughters.

He was proud of his knowledge of English, especially the English Classics. He named all of his sons after either the titles or the authors of the English Classics.

He had a philosophy that some may call unusual. For example, I heard him say that this country started downhill when women were given the right to vote and when prohibition was repealed.

He contended that women are too emotional to make rational decisions on leadership and that alcohol consumption was more fun when you had to sneak around to buy and drink it.

He practiced what he preached by hiding his bottle in the barn. I suspect this was due mostly to the fact that my grandmother would not allow alcohol in the house. He would often announce that he was going to the barn to tend the livestock. He had the most cared for livestock in the area.

I suspect that my grandmother knew what he was doing but decided that he should have his "fun".

My paternal Grandfather (second from the left) and his students.

MATERNAL GRANDFATHER

My maternal grandfather was a small, thin man. He was smaller and much thinner than my grandmother.

He was a master carpenter who bought a log house and added on to it whenever a child was born. He ended up with a rather large house.

Hand tools were all he used in his carpentry. When we visited, I was always warned to never touch his tools because he did not want them to be "out of whack". (I guess his tools were always "in whack").

He was an avid hunter and his favorite sport was turkey hunting. Turkeys were scarce. When the season was open, he would take his gun, supplies and sleeping equipment to the woods and stay until he got a turkey. This could take two or three days during which he camped in the forest.

My Little Tin Horn

My Maternal Grandfather

My Paternal Grandmother

DINNER AT MY GRANDPARENTS

Some weekends we would visit my grandparents unannounced. The most amazing thing about those visits was that my grandmothers were able to put together a huge meal even on a short notice. The meals would include several main courses (chicken, ham, and beef), many side dishes and two or three desserts (my favorite part).

Sometimes, one or more of my uncles and/or aunts would be there. With their children there would be more people than could be seated at the table. This would result in the men being fed first. There would be additional seating after the men were finished. The women and children would eat from what was left.

A CHANGE

When World War II ended my father sold the small farm and bought a much larger one in an adjoining county. This was another big change in my life.

CHAPTER 3

After World War II

THE NEW FARM

The new farm was where I spent my late childhood and teen years. The property had about five hundred acres that included farmland, pastureland, and woodland. It was located about two miles from a small town.

The farm was not used during the war years and had grown tall grass and weeds. Rabbits were plentiful and hunting them was great sport. However, this habitat was gone after we had done much work in reclaiming the fields and pastures.

We started farming with horses but after the first year they were sold and my father bought a tractor. By the time I was about eight years old, I had learned to drive it. When I was about ten or eleven I had learned to drive a pickup truck and a cattle truck.

A NEW SCHOOL

Shortly after our move to the new farm I entered a new school. It was HUGE! It was two stories high and each grade contained more students than the entire school I had previously attended! There were eight or nine buses that brought both elementary and high school students from every direction. I did not know there were that many kids in the whole world! I wondered where they came from.

The farmhouse where I spent my late youth and teen years.

THE LITTLE BROWN-HAIRED GIRL

In a short time I settled down in the fourth grade and began my new adventures.

I was assigned a seat near the middle of the classroom. I noticed a vacant seat one row to the right and one seat up. After about a week I asked the student sitting behind me about it. He told me it belonged to a little brown-haired girl who was out sick. His exact words were, "She is the prettiest girl in our class".

A few weeks after her return, she became my nemesis. I don't know why this happened. Maybe it was because I was very shy. One day the teacher left the room and the girl announced she was going to kiss me.

Talk about fear! No way was I going to let this happen. I ran up the aisle, across the front of the room, down the side of the room, through the cloakroom, and all around. I was scared to death and ran lap after lap.

I soon became the "sport of choice". The little brown-haired girl began assigning other girls the fun of chasing me. (Some years later, when I played sports in high school, my coach would say that I should run faster because the girls were almost as fast as me. The operative word was "almost").

This "sport" continued throughout the fifth grade and into the sixth. One day the little red-haired girl was assigned to be the chaser.

I was running lap number two and I got to thinking. I thought about what I had read and seen in magazines or comic books where the "hero" kisses the girl and seems to enjoy it. So, I decided to give it a try. On lap number three, I turned in the cloakroom, caught the girl and kissed her.

That was the end of the chasing. I have always wondered if it stopped because I was a bad kisser or a good kisser.

KILLER

In the sixth grade, two of the kids in my class thought it was great fun to sneak up behind me and stuff shelled corn down my shirt collar.

This went on for some time until I got fed up with it. One noon hour I sensed one of them coming up behind me and swung a right cross while turning around. I couldn't have timed it better. I made a solid hit to the bridge of his nose and thought I had killed him because he hit the ground and didn't make a move. I ran to the restroom to await the sheriff and be arrested.

After about ten minutes the "dead" kid came into the bathroom to wipe the blood off his nose.

Those kids never stuffed corn down my shirt collar again.

THE LONE RANGER

My favorite radio program was "The Lone Ranger" which came on near dark once a week. The program promoted what was called "The Lone Ranger Safety Club". Three or four of us at school decided to join. The requirement to join was to send in three wrappers from Mertia Bread and to recommend Merita Bread to three housewives. The other kids and I just gave the names of the others' mothers (without asking their approval).

About two weeks after I sent in the required material, I received my silver "Ranger" star and became an official member of the Lone Ranger Safety Club. What a proud day that was!

I earned other items but the only one I can remember was a "Silver Bullet" pencil sharpener.

THE SNOWSTORM

One year, I believe I was in the sixth grade, a large snowstorm occurred between Christmas and New Year's. No traffic could move on the roads and snowplows were unable to cut through the drifts. Snowdrifts were so deep that only a few fence posts were showing.

There was no school for about a week after the New Year. With larger equipment, the roads were opened and school buses could travel.

SLED RIDING

I always had a sled that was shared with my sister and brother. We always looked forward to the first snow of the year and hoped it was deep enough to sled ride. There were several steep hills on our farm where we could ride for a considerable distance.

The biggest problem going down the hill was that you had to drag the sled back uphill. Thus, it didn't take long to get tired of sled riding.

Another problem was that, after the snow had melted and refrozen, a hard crust formed on top of the snow. The speed of the sled was greatly increased. Sometimes the sled would break through the crust and stop suddenly. You didn't. This resulted in skinned arms, face, and etcetera.

NO BIRTHDAY CAKE

Late one summer, just three days before my birthday, my second brother was born. A couple of weeks later my mother remembered that she had not made a cake for my birthday. With all the excitement, I had also forgotten it.

Shelton R. McKeever

BB AMMO

One of my friends at school and I were discussing our BB guns when I told him I was out of ammo. He asked if my father had shotgun shells and I said yes. He told me that those shells had BB's inside.

I found out after going through several different boxes that only some of the BB's were the correct size.

When I finished several shotgun shells, I had to find a place for the shell casings. I finally decided that the best place was in the coal shed under a pile of coal.

Our house had two sources of heat during the winter. The first was a wood-burning kitchen stove. The other was a coal-burning potbellied stove in the living room.

One cold evening, as the family was gathered in the living room, there was a loud "WHOOSH" as the stove door flew open and a cloud of smoke and soot filled the room. I realized immediately what had happened. However, my father blamed it on the coal company, saying that they had left dynamite caps in the coal.

This happened a second time so my father looked carefully at the ashes and found brass from the shell casings. He looked directly at me and asked if I knew what that was. Of course I didn't know. After some "reminding" my memory improved.

RAIN SHELTER

One afternoon, while walking through a back field, I was surprised by a thunderstorm. I was quite a distance from our house and the only shelter was under the overhang of a hay stack.

I pushed backwards under the overhang and managed to stay dry during the downpour.

The rain quit after about fifteen minutes and I eased myself away from the hay stack. Something made me look back and I saw a snake about two feet from where I had been sitting. I did not linger to see if the snake was harmless or not.

WINTER CHURCH SERVICES

In the winter, church services were interesting.

Most of the men in the community were farmers. They would rise before daylight, dress in their heavy clothing and go out through the cold and snow to feed their livestock. They would then go back to their house to clean up, put on their "Sunday clothes", and have a heavy breakfast.

After breakfast they would go to church, which was kept fairly warm. Within minutes they would be asleep. I would look around and see ten or eleven men of the church sound asleep.

The most interesting thing was that, during the following week, two or three men would gather. They would talk about and laugh at those that had fallen asleep.

The next Sunday it would be them that were asleep.

HOEING CORN

The most thankless and tiring job on the farm was to hoe the cornfield.

One cornfield was very long and required much manual labor. My father, brother and I would go to the field after breakfast and hoe to the far end and back. Then, it was time to go to dinner (lunch). After dinner, it was back to the field to do the same thing. Then it was time for supper (dinner).

This required about two weeks of work to finish the field. Then, we started all over again.

Shelton R. McKeever

STORING APPLES AND CABBAGES

The technique we used to store apples and cabbage for the winter was to bury them under a mound of leaves and soil.

Apples were placed on a pile of leaves and covered with more leaves. Then, dirt was piled on top of that to a depth of one to two feet. A drainage ditch was dug around this pile. During the winter we would go to the pile, dig into it and get our apples.

Cabbage was stored the same way but it was important that they be pulled out of the ground, root and all, and stored with the roots pointed upward.

CANNING VEGETABLES

When the vegetables ripened in the garden, we would quit work in the fields and devote all our time to harvesting and canning them. When the tomatoes ripened, my main job was to do the picking. Sometimes I would join in on peeling them.

We did the same thing when the sweet corn ripened.

This canning would take almost a week for each crop. The pressure cooker would be going from daylight to late at night.

SOFT DRINKS

From time to time my father would take cattle to market or go to the market to purchase livestock. The market was about forty miles from our house and it took considerable time to travel over the mountain roads.

On the way home in the evening my father would stop along the way and buy me a soft drink. The first one I had was when I was about ten years old. This was a real treat.

I never decided if I liked grape or orange the best.

ELECTRICITY

When I was about eleven years old, electrical lines were extended through our farm. My fathered hired an electrician to wire the house.

We discovered that the house, which was built in 1812, had been insulated with wheat and oat husks. We would drill holes for the wires and these husks would pour out.

That wiring would not even come close to passing present day requirements.

There was a bare overhead light bulb and two or three wall sockets in each room. However, these lights were a great improvement over the kerosene lamps we were using. Also, for the first time, we now had a refrigerator and electrical stove. Later, my mother bought a washer and dryer.

Shelton R. McKeever

TELEPHONE SERVICE

We had no telephone until several years after electrical power became available. This service was the crank-type telephone. We were on a party line where each household had a different signal. (One long and one short, or two shorts, or three longs, etc). The telephone operator would connect you to other party lines for those calls not on your line.

OUT HOUSE

We had no inside "plumbing". When necessary, taking a trip behind the house was in order.

During the winter in sub-freezing weather the trip was something you did not look forward to. To keep the pain to a minimum, you waited until the last minute to make a dash for it. You finished as soon as possible and made a dash back to the house.

The outhouse was not a permanent fixture. After a few years, it was necessary to build a new structure at a different location. There was always the danger of getting up in the middle of the night half asleep and trying to visit the old location.

MOVIES

One Saturday, when I was about twelve years old, my father announced that he was taking all of us to the movie at the county seat.

This was a surprise and a shock. I had seen only two movies before this. The first time was when I was very young and I went with my parents. The only thing I remember was seeing a cowboy jump from his horse to a moving train. Amazing!

The other one was also a "western" when my father left me there while he was conducting business at a nearby building.

The name of this movie was "A Night at the Opera" with the Marx Brothers. I had never seen anything as funny as that movie. For many years, I wanted to see it again. I got my chance a few years ago when I saw it on late night TV. It was not as funny as I remembered.

COUNTY SEAT SATURDAY NIGHTS

After the first movie trip, it became a family routine to go to the county seat on Saturday nights at least twice a month. Many families from throughout the county also did this.

I always looked forward to seeing a movie on Saturday night. By the way, when you went to a movie, you paid for admission and went in and sat down. It made no difference if the movie had begun or not. Sometimes it was half over when you got there. In any case, you could watch it to the end and back to where you came in.

People would gather for the movies. Some had other activities. The women would spread the latest gossip. The men would discuss their livestock and crops then many would meet at the pool hall. Teenage boys would woo the teenage girls and vice versa. After the movie, I would sometimes get to go to the drugstore for a soda or a banana split.

Saturday nights were something I really looked forward to.

Shelton R. McKeever

NIGHT OF THE "FLASH"

One summer night, just after bedtime, there was a bright "flash" that lit up the sky. There were many reports from throughout the area that Martians had landed.

For several nights after that, I slept with my head under the covers. Actually, I did not break myself of that habit until I was about eighteen years old.

ROTTEN EGGS

There were chickens living in the barn which was located about two hundred yards from our house. These chickens would make nests in the hay. Sometimes, a nest or two was covered when additional hay was stored.

Ever so often my older brother and I would uncover one or more nests while feeding the cattle. The eggs had been there for considerable time and were rotten. This gave us the opportunity to get into an egg throwing battle. This was usually very innocent and we were able to take shelter behind piles of hay.

One day, during one of these battles, I calculated that if I threw to the roof over his head he would get splattered with rotten egg. I did and it worked.

I had to explain to my parents what I had done.

ROCK CLIMBING

A small cliff, which was about twenty feet high, was located on our farm. One day, as my brother and I walked up to it I said "let's climb it". Before I knew what was happening, he began to climb.

There was no way he was going to outdo me. So I began to climb also. I don't know how we did it but we made it to the top.

That was the end of my rock-climbing career.

BEANS

From time to time my mother would make my favorite meal. This consisted of a pot of pinto beans cooked with a slab of ham.

The beans were eaten with a sliced tomato, sliced onion, horseradish and cornbread. Talk about good! This is still one of my favorite meals.

The only hazard with this meal is that it can make one socially unacceptable.

4-H CLUB

Many of the farm children in the area belonged to the 4-H Club. The local club meetings were held about once a month and were enjoyable with games and refreshments.

Special countywide events were also held. These events included daylong meetings and presentations. Once a year a "field day" was held which included athletic and crop judging contests.

Emphasis of the club was on farm and household activities and projects. Each member had to adopt a project to be conducted during the year.

My project was to raise a "baby beef". The object was to purchase a young calf and raise and train it to a yearling (one year +).

I had to feed, groom and teach it to be led on a rope halter. I also had to train it to be shown at fairs. This required at least an hour a day of practice.

I usually took the calf to the county and state fair. This meant that the calf was penned in a fair barn for about four days. During this time, I would sleep on my cot in the barn loft (along

with other kids who had animals for showing).
I would eat sandwiches, hot dogs and soft
drinks (fair food). This was a lot of fun.

My daily activity during the fair was to feed
the calf early in the morning. Then I would lead
it to an area where it was washed, dried and the
hair curled or waved. While the calf dried off, I
would clean the pen and bring in new straw.

Judging usually took place on the evening of
the second or third day. I would march the calf
around the show room along with about twenty
others. At the end of the competition the judges
would award ribbons: blue for first place, red
for second, green for third. I usually won one of
these.

In the fall, there would be a final show
followed by the sale of my calf. Some might
think it was a sad time but I never thought
about it. A couple of weeks later I would
acquire another calf and start all over again.

THE YELLOWJACKET NEST

One afternoon my mother sent me to the garden to pick green beans for dinner. About half way down a row I noticed a nest of yellow jackets and had to detour around them.

Once I returned to the house the thought occurred to me that the nest needed to be destroyed. After considering several alternatives I decided that they could be burned out.

I siphoned a pint of gasoline from the tractor tank, took a box of kitchen matches and headed back to the garden. With the match in my right hand and the gasoline in my left hand I approached the nest. I quickly doused the nest with the gasoline and struck the match and flung it toward the nest.

WHOOSH!

I learned my first lesson about gasoline: It's the vapors that burn, not the liquid. Of course there were vapors in front of my face.

I had created another problem. How to explain the absence of eyebrows and eyelashes? I considered telling my parents that the sun was too hot or that I had worked so hard that I burned them off. Both those lies were unbelievable so I decided to tell the truth.

When I told my parents, all my father said was for me to make sure the tractor gas tank was filled again. (Lesson two about gasoline: Refill the tank you used).

FAVORITE TIME AND PLACE

In the winter, during a heavy snowfall, I enjoyed walking in the woods to a favorite spot. This spot was a large hemlock tree that had branches reaching the ground.

I would sit with my back against the tree trunk and watch the snow through the branches. During this time the birds and all other wildlife had found shelter and there was no sound except for the soft tapping of snowflakes on the leaves.

It's hard to explain how peaceful I found this to be. This made me realize that we are all one with nature and that God created everything to be as one.

THE ALCOHOLIC

There were a couple of small apple orchards on the farm. In the early fall, we would borrow a cider press and process apple juice.

Several gallon jugs of juice would be stored in a springhouse located a short distance from our house. After working in the fields all day, a cup of cool juice tasted mighty good. It was a daily ritual to go to the springhouse after work for the apple juice.

One of my chores in the evening was to find the milk cows in the pasture and bring them back to be milked.

One evening as I set out and passed the springhouse, I remembered that it had been a week or so since I had a drink of apple juice. So, I stopped and had a cup that tasted so good I had a second and third cup. I did notice that the juice tasted a little funny but thought nothing of it (then).

I continued my walk to the pasture. After a while I noticed that the cows were located in a different direction. I changed directions until I noticed that they were not in that direction.

This went on for a considerable time until I finally managed to get the cows home.

Needless to say, I had the grand tour of several pastures. It was later that I learned the cider had become "hard" (fermented).

THE NOT-SO-GREAT SMOKEOUT

Sometime during the early spring of sixth grade two of my classmates and I decided that we were grown up enough to smoke cigarettes. We decided to save a nickel each from our lunch money. After a couple of days we would have enough to purchase a twenty-five cent package of Camels.

I was elected as the one to walk about two blocks and make the purchase. Because the store owner and my father were good friends, I imagine that my parents knew about my purchase before I got back to school. However nothing was ever said.

The next problem we had to overcome was to find a place to smoke in secret. Across the street from the schoolhouse was an old farmstead with a vacant barn. This turned out to be a perfect place. We stashed the pack of cigarettes in a crack of the barn.

We could not have made a better choice (or worse depending upon one's point of view) than Camels. I can't forget that first puff. There we were - three young boys coughing and wheezing and on the verge of throwing up. It's a wonder the whole town didn't hear us. We were almost finished with the pack before we could take a puff without the after effects.

Every second or third day the three of us would sneak across the street and have our noon time smoke. We were into our second pack when another student got wise by following us to the barn. He threatened to tell on us if we did not let him have a "free smoke".

My two pals and I decided that this could get out of hand and become expensive. Therefore, we needed to "break the habit" and not buy any more cigarettes.

CHAPTER 4

Facts Learned the Hard Way

There were many things that I learned during my youth. Many of them are applicable today. They include the following:

Don't walk on your mother's clean floor. Wait until it is dirty to walk on it.

After coming in from the rain, don't sit in your father's favorite chair in your wet clothes. (For that matter don't sit in your mother's favorite chair either).

If you are caught outside during a thunderstorm, don't take shelter under a haystack. Snakes don't like to get wet either.

Don't hide in the tool shed when there is digging, hoeing or shoveling work to be done.

After the work is done make sure you have dusted the straw off your clothes or your father will discover your hiding place in the barn.

If the girl who sits in front of you in the schoolroom is bigger, stronger, or faster than you – don't pull her hair. If she is all of the above, don't even think about it.

Don't pick a fight with the school bully unless you bring along a couple of friends that are slower runners than you.

Don't pick a fight with a kid who has two brothers and ten cousins standing around him.

Don't tell your best buddy that you like a certain girl unless you want everyone in school to know about it. Don't tell that girl he is no longer your best buddy unless you want everyone in school to know about it.

Don't walk through the barnyard in your new shoes.

Don't walk on thin ice while wearing your father's new wool sweater.

Don't cross a stream on an ice-covered log. For that matter, don't cross a stream on any log. They are very unstable.

Don't let your sister touch a push lawnmower while you are cleaning grass from the blades. For that matter, don't clean the blades if she is anywhere within the county.

Don't pick up a dropped item in front of a buck sheep.

Don't wear red clothing in front of a bull.

When you are cleaning out the barn and using a manure spreader to scatter it over a field, don't look back to see how things are going. (It's much better to take a "splat" on the back of the head than on the front).

If you don't know the depth of a snowdrift, let your brother or sister go first.

Don't bring home a "bad" report card or your parents will make you study an extra two hours to improve your grades. Also, don't bring home a "good" report card or your parents will make you study an extra two hours to maintain your grades.

Don't poke a hornet's nest with a short stick. (Use a long one).

If telling the truth will get you spanked, tell a real good lie. You will enjoy the spanking more (maybe).

If you can't swim, don't wade in deep water.

Don't go out on a limb if it doesn't support your weight.

Don't play on the roof while wearing slick shoes.

You can lose one or more shoes while wading in deep mud.

Believe your mother when she tells you that she has planted some very hot peppers in the garden. Disbelief can burn your tongue off.

LaVergne, TN USA
14 March 2011
219996LV00001B/1/P